THE ALCOHOLIC HUSBAND PRIMER

Survival Tips For The Alcoholic's Wife

by

Wren Waters

INTRODUCTION

There is in every true woman's heart, a spark of heavenly fire, which lies dormant in the broad daylight of prosperity, but which kindles up and beams and blazes in the dark hour of adversity.

Washington Irving

When I married my husband in 2001, I had no idea he was an alcoholic. I knew he drank a little too much but I most certainly did not know - or even think - he was an alcoholic. Anyway, it would have made no difference had I known. I was shockingly, blissfully ignorant as to what alcoholism really was and the depravity with which it manifests itself in human beings. Now, over 15 years later and fully indoctrinated into The Life (of an alcoholic's wife), I am surprised at how insulated I was from the realities of alcoholism. How I spent the first 35+ years of my life untouched by this tragically common affliction, I don't know. But I do know the minute my husband and I returned home from our honeymoon, the beast of alcoholism was hell-bent on bringing me up to speed.

My husband and I had dated for more than two years before tying the knot but it wasn't until we were married that I came to see the full scope, i.e. the sheer volume, of his drinking. It's not that I turned a blind eye to his imbibing while we were dating; it's just my husband-to-be, like any alcoholic worth his weight in booze, was well schooled at hiding the true nature and extent of his drinking.

Temporarily anyway. Once you are living under the same roof as the alcoholic, no matter how much he may want to, he can no longer hide his truth. In the early months of our marriage, I (naively) confronted him about his drinking. He (naturally) defended himself.

"But who drinks eight or nine or TEN of anything in one night," I'd ask in the way of a rebuttal to his justifications. That, along with anything and everything else I said on the subject, fell on deaf, often intoxicated, ears.

Empty beer bottles littered my kitchen counter. Empty beers cans were stashed in desk drawers. During the winter months, cases of beer stood outside the backdoor, chilling in the cold night air. Anywhere and everywhere I turned there was evidence. Still he denied it. Still it nagged at me.

Somehow we managed to limp along for the first seven or eight years of our marriage.

We had children. I ignored the empties.

We made love. I forgave his drunken, emotionally vacant days.

We lived like a happy family. I pretended it was all true.

And then in 2009 something happened.

Everything that had been festering and brewing, percolating and stewing, churning and gurgling beneath the surface erupted like an emotional Mt. Vesuvius.

The molten lava and volcanic ash of an alcoholic marriage rained down upon my life.

It's not as though 2009 was the *first* time my husband called me a fucking bitch or told me to shut the fuck up. It's just it was (apparently) the first time that I realized - or acknowledge, I'm not sure which - that I had a problem, a very *big problem,* on my hands.

Still, another five years seemed to just disappear without me doing anything more than simply enduring the pain, frustration and isolation of life with an alcoholic husband. This isn't a commentary on me or any other woman who is married to an alcoholic and finds five, ten or more years of her life have slipped away. It's easy to lose the years when you are working hard to survive the days.

But then one night after one of my husband's uglier – though certainly not atypical – verbal assaults, I decided I could no longer live by simply *enduring* my life... my marriage... my husband. I could not continue to deny and pretend what was happening in my life and my home was not happening in my life and home. I needed to open up. To someone. Anyone. I needed to go in search of resources, guidance and support that was for *me,* the wife of an alcoholic.

I never suspected finding such would not be easy.

Few things in the world can make a woman feel as utterly alone and completely dejected as being called a fucking bitch, told to shut the fuck up and/or wished upon to fucking die by the man she married.

My husband would say these horrible, vicious things to me.

And then go to bed.

Me?

I was left sitting up in the middle of the night crying. The quiet darkness of the house adding its own layer of pain. I wanted to find resources, guidance and support but I had no idea where to look. And even if I did know where to look, I wasn't even sure what it was I was looking for. What did I want? What was I hoping, expecting to find? What would the resources, guidance and support I was searching for even look like anyway?

I started at the only natural place – for the 21st century that is – there is to start: the Internet. I googled "alcoholic's wife," "wife of alcoholic," "alcoholic husband" and other assorted sundries on the same theme. I thought, subconsciously at least, that since there are countless facilities and programs, blogs and websites devoted to the alcoholic, it would be equally so for the wife of an alcoholic. After all, don't they say alcoholism is a family disease?

Well, it may be a "family disease" but looking back I realize it was naive of me to expect that the recovery and medical communities devote the same amount of energy and attention to the alcoholic's wife and family as to the alcoholic himself. The truth is that the alcoholic's family, and in particular his wife, is poorly represented in the support communities. It seems to me that the wives of alcoholics are seen more as *extensions of* their husbands' drinking rather than as individuals with their own unique and valid needs. Most of the advice offered to the woman living with an alcoholic husband is alcoholic-centric. It is predicated on the idea that she can somehow help or support him. At the very least, she should be able to address, change and/or fix her own flawed behavior that is contributing to or exacerbating his drinking. The idea (fact?) that she is a victim of his drinking, not a co-conspirator *in* his drinking, does not seem to be widely supported in the recovery community.

So rather than ferreting out the guidance and support I was craving, my late-night googling efforts were uncovering a void in that said support and guidance. Now finally aware of what it was I was looking for, I realized it really wasn't out there. Not that I could find anyway.

But for some reason, I didn't quit. Whether out anger, frustration, loneliness or simply the need to do *something,* no matter how futile it was proving, I was determined to reach beyond myself and the emotional confines of my alcoholic marriage. I could feel in me a visceral-like need to connect with women like myself. Women I knew must be out there considering alcoholism is the number one drug problem in the United States.

There are an estimated 15 MILLION alcoholics!

Of those 15 million, I was pretty sure lots of them had wives.

Eventually my perseverance did pay off.

Since that fateful period in my life, I have met many women who are dealing with the fall out of living with a compulsive drinker. Everything from blogs to Al Anon to serendipitous meetings while standing in line at the grocery store or changing in the locker room at the gym (odd what conversations come up when you're standing half naked in front of another woman who is half-naked) has connected me with women just like myself. Women who are warm, caring, kind, creative but also suffering and struggling. Women who are working hard to navigate life with an alcoholic husband.

In the beginning, I was the beginner. The fledgling. The amateur. The one who so desperately craved advice, information, enlightenment and understanding on the complexities and idiosyncrasies of alcoholism.

Until one day I wasn't.

Until one day I was no longer the confused and dazed one.

I was no longer the one wondering how it was my husband could be acting this way.

I was no longer the one who needed the truth about alcoholism explained to her.

I wasn't the one crying on someone else's shoulder.

One day I had become *the one*...

Consoling the confused and dazed.

Explaining how it was her husband could be acting "this way."

Trying to offer comfort in the way of logical explanations for illogical behavior and choices.

I was the shoulder being cried upon.

The sad reality (or one of the many sad realities anyway) of alcoholism is all alcoholics are the same just in different ways. No alcoholic husband seems to behave in exactly the same manner and yet what is driving the behavior - the science and physiology behind the behavior - is the same for one alcoholic as it is for another as it is for another.

In time, I began to hear myself explaining the same things over and over again to many different women. One day the writer in me bolted awake and yelled,

"HEY! Why don't you write a book for women who are just becoming aware of what it means to be married to an alcoholic?!"

OK, maybe that's not really what the writer in me said. Maybe it was more like,

"Hey! Why don't you write a book about how to deal with your husband if he is an alcoholic prick?"

Either way, the writer in me did bolt awake and while the only thing she really wants to say is,

"RUN! RUN NOW! RUN FAR AND FAST AND DON'T LOOK BACK!"

She (and I) know that isn't always possible or even desirable. (Plus, it would make for a very short book.)

So instead I decided to be a little more thorough and put together in one place (i.e. this book) some of the most basic and fundamental survival tips I have garnished along the way. Of course, there is nothing basic or fundamental about being married to an alcoholic. It's infinitely complex with the magnitude and depth of an alcoholic's pathology nearly incomprehensible - even when you are living it on a daily basis.

Or perhaps especially when you are living it on a daily basis.

To live with an alcoholic husband is to live on the sea - a tumultuous, hostile sea that swells with waves of toxicity and insanity. There is no easy way to navigate these waters but perhaps there is at least an *easier* way. I hope these tips help.

16 Survival Tips for the Alcoholic's Wife

1. Really understand what alcoholism is. The alcoholic can't promise his way sober.

2. Know the difference between not drinking and being sober.

3. Realize nothing will be solved if he "just" quits drinking.

4. AA is the answer. AA is NOT the answer.

5. Al-Anon is the answer. Al-Anon is NOT the answer.

6. Beware the "recovering" alcoholic.

7. Know that he WILL get worse. Alcoholism is a progressive disorder.

8. Know that the alcoholic projects his worse fears, his greatest self-loathing and his darkest darkness onto you, his wife.

9. The alcoholic knows he has a problem.

10. Learn how to recognize when he's baiting you - and how to NOT take it!

11. Do yourself a favor: don't look for or throw out his alcohol stash.

12. Come to expect NOTHING of your alcoholic husband.

13. Leaving isn't always the answer. One day leaving is the only answer.

14. Most likely he will NOT leave you.

15. There IS a point of no return.

16. And finally...

17. Create your own reality. Or your alcoholic husband will create it for you.

The Scorpion and the Frog

One day a scorpion needed to cross a wide, raging river. Seeing a frog about to take the journey, he asked the frog,

"Will you take me across the river?".

The frog, well aware of the scorpion's legendary and deadly sting, said, "No, I most certainly will not. You will sting me and I will die.

But the scorpion replied, "Why would I sting you? Then we would both die."

This seemed logical and obvious enough so the frog agreed to carry the scorpion across the river. The scorpion climbed onto the frog's back but just when they had reached the middle of the river, the scorpion did, indeed, sting the frog.

As they were both drowning, the frog cried, "Why did you do that?! Now we are both going to die."

To which the scorpion answered, "It is my nature..."

SURVIVAL TIP #1

Really Understand What Alcoholism Is

I can't tell you how many times the wife of an alcoholic has said to me, desperation and disbelief dripping from her voice, "My husband promised he'd stop drinking but he's started again."

You don't necessarily need to understand all the physiology, chemistry and brain science of alcoholism to survive marriage to an alcoholic but a general understanding, even a sort of begrudging appreciation for what alcoholism is can help alleviate some of your frustration. Ok, it probably can't. It's hard to alleviate the frustration of living with an alcoholic. None the less, you still need to avail yourself of a basic, fact-based understanding of what alcoholism is and what you are really dealing with. If you hope to have any chance at preserving your own sanity, that is.

ALCOHOLICS CANNOT - CANNOT, CANNOT, CANNOT!!! - PROMISE THEMSELVES SOBER. IF THEY COULD, THEY WOULDN'T BE ALCOHOLICS!

It doesn't matter how earnestly the alcoholic promises. It doesn't matter how sick he gets, how many jobs he loses or even if he stands in the living room pissing himself night after night. It doesn't matter how much you beg, how much the kids beg or how often a judge threatens.

IT DOESN'T MATTER IF HE STANDS TO LOSE HIS JOB, HIS HOUSE, HIS WIFE, HIS KIDS, HIS MONEY, HIS FREEDOM. IT DOESN'T MATTER IF HE'S ABOUT TO DESTROY EVERYTHING THAT IS OF ANY VALUE AND IMPORTANCE IN HIS LIFE, YOUR LIFE, HIS KIDS' LIVES.

IT WOULDN'T EVEN MATTER IF IT WAS HIS OWN MOTHER'S HEAD ON THE CHOPPING BLOCK!!

THE ALCOHOLIC CAN NOT WILL HIMSELF TO STOP DRINKING COMPULSIVELY.

THAT'S WHY HE'S AN ALCOHOLIC!

So when he promises - no matter how often he promises, no matter how impassioned or vehement those promises may be, no matter how many days or even weeks he upholds his promises - do not (do not, do not, DO NOT!) be surprised, disappointed or hurt when he resumes drinking.

THE ALCOHOLIC DOES NOT SPONTANEOUSLY ACHIEVE SOBRIETY.

This is not a commentary on you. It's not a commentary on how much he loves you or values your marriage. It's not a commentary on what his children mean to him, how smart he is, how moral he is or how badly he wants to remain clean.

IT'S A COMMENTARY ON THE VERY NATURE OF ALCOHOLISM AND WHAT IT MEANS TO BE AN ALCOHOLIC.

The alcoholic who attempts a self-imposed, promise-based sobriety is going to start drinking again. Oh, I know. Your neighbor's cousin's wife's Uncle Fred drank for 50 years and then one day said he'd never drink again

And he hasn't touched a drop since!

And that was 25 years ago.

Well, legendary sobriety stories not-with-standing, alcoholics stand virtually no chance of maintaining sobriety based on promises. And the alcoholic who participates in a professional recovery program? I hate to tell you (though I must); those recovery rates are rather dismal as well.

A man who drinks too much on occasion is still the man he was sober. An alcoholic, a real alcoholic, is not the same at all. You can't predict anything about him for sure except that he will be someone you have never met before.

Raymond Chandler

The Long Goodbye

SURVIVAL TIP #2

Know The Difference Between Not Drinking And Being Sober

To the layman and uninitiated, Not Drinking and Being Sober appear to be the same thing. But the fact is, Not Drinking and Being Sober are two very distinct and different states of being.

Early on in my education of living with an alcoholic, I met a woman at the gym who was a recovering alcoholic herself. Why or how we came to reveal our secrets to one another within ten minutes of meeting is perhaps one of those mysteries of serendipity. (Or the result of the oxygen deprivation we were each experiencing due to our efforts to keep up with our 28-year-old, body-like-a-Greek-God, Zumba instructor). Either way, I told her my husband was an alcoholic and that there were times when I *knew* he hadn't been drinking and yet he was just as moody, hostile, volatile, combative and angry as when he was drinking.

"That's called a 'dry drunk,'" she said, not at all surprised at the description of my husband's behavior.

A dry drunk is just as the phrase suggests: all the lovely hostility, aggression, anger, resentment, selfishness, etc., etc., etc. without the benefit or need of alcohol!

The reason for this is twofold:

First, as the alcoholism progresses in the alcoholic (and it always progresses; see Tip #7), thoughts of drinking, when he can drink again and/or where he is going to get that drink begin to consume his daily thinking. So when you two are at your kid's parent-teacher conference, or shopping for a new sofa or you're explaining to him why the plumber needs to replace all the plumbing in the bathroom, what he's really thinking is:

16

when will this conference be over, pick a damn couch already and please shut up about plumbing...so I can go get a drink!

I'm not here to defend the alcoholic's behavior. But I am trying to explain it a little. The need and craving for alcohol comes to consume the alcoholic's thoughts.

And then! As if to tie it all up with a nice, big red raging bow, is the fact (fact!) that alcohol is a poison. And the sustained excessive and compulsive ingesting of said poison causes brain damage.

And not just any old brain damage.

Not brain damage in some remote corner of the brain where it's hardly noticed. Or where the brain can repair itself. Or where another part of the brain can be brought into play to compensate for said damage. This isn't baseball. There's no call to the bull pen to save the game.

Alcohol damages the frontal lobe of the brain!

Of course, it affects and harms and damages the human body in a whole host of ways that go way beyond just the brain but in terms of understanding alcohol's effects on the alcoholic's behavior – and the subsequent changes (i.e. worsening) in the alcoholic's behavior over the years - let's just stick with this:

Sustained compulsive drinking DAMAGES the FRONTAL LOBE of the HUMAN BRAIN!

And guess what the "frontal lobe" of the human brain is responsible for? Oh, you know, all sorts of good things like judgment and impulse control. The alcoholic's brain is under constant assault from his excessive drinking. The effects don't go away simply because he hasn't had a drink for a few hours, days or even weeks. That's why being Sober or sustaining Sobriety is not the same as simply Not Drinking.

The definition of sober is "not affected by alcohol."

The definition is not "not affected by alcohol recently drank."

The alcoholic can go weeks without actually drinking alcohol and still, sadly, be profoundly affected by it. It's a physical thing! The alcoholic's brain is being physically changed (i.e. damaged!) to where it becomes increasingly unable to function as a healthy organ. So even though your husband may abstain from drinking one night, one week-end, several days or even longer, don't expect a great change in his behavior. And beware, the longer he drinks, the more regular his dry drunks become. In other words, the dry drunk behavior - moodiness, anger, hostility - slowly, tragically evolves (devolves?) into his new-normal while his once healthy- normal behavior and disposition is systematically edged out.

Like so many addicts, I'd thought that if I could only sort out my life, I could sort out my drinking. It was a revelation to see that it would be simpler the other way around.

Peter Townshend

Who I Am

SURVIVAL TIP #3

Realize Nothing Will Be Solved If He "Just" Quits Drinking

Since not drinking and being sober are two entirely different states of being, know that even if your husband could "just" quit drinking, not much would change or be fixed without him seeking professional therapy or treatment for his addiction. Many treatment and therapy programs are predicated on the idea that alcoholism is a secondary morbidity. That is, something else was wrong *first* that drove the not-yet-alcoholic to drink to excess. But the truth is sustained compulsive drinking, i.e. alcoholism, causes a whole host of problems, all on its own, that need to be fixed and addressed if there is to be true sobriety *and* a successful marriage. My husband could quit drinking *tomorrow* and really nothing would change between us. The amount of anger and hostility, resentment and even his own guilt – over his drinking and the associated behavior - would continue to flow through our lives like nuclear run off in the ground water. And so when I realized that without addressing these issues, without professional help really, it *didn't matter* whether my husband quit drinking or not, I felt as if someone had locked me in a prison.

While simultaneously setting me free!

On one hand, it was completely devastating to realize that hanging my hat of hope on my husband "just not drinking" was futile and useless. Like being in the desert and finally reaching that glistening puddle of water – only to discover it is a mirage - my belief that all my husband had to do was not drink was its own mirage. Even if he did quit drinking - and there was little hope of that - he would be just as angry and hostile as when drinking if he didn't seek professional help. And that was even less-likely than him giving up alcohol! No, I wasn't getting out of this that easily.

And yet, because there was no point in hoping for that, I was liberated from a lifetime of wishing for, wanting and waiting on something that was a) probably not coming and b) wouldn't deliver the hoped-for results even if it did arrive.

The solution to your husband's drinking problem lies far, far beyond him simply never taking another drink. Depending on how long he has been drinking compulsively and obsessively, some of the damage might not be able to be un-done.

And even if your husband does quit drinking, even if he maintains his sobriety, (see Tip #2) it doesn't necessarily mean he is going to understand or take responsibility for the kind of searing pain his drinking has caused you and your family. My sister-in-law is a recovering alcoholic (whom I must add I am very proud of for the hard, tough road she is travelling) and she tells me that she hears over and over again from recovering-alcoholic husbands,

"I quit drinking and she's still mad."

Or, "I quit drinking and she still left. What does she want?"

Well, of course what we want is for the demon to be exorcised completely. We want our husbands to quit drinking, change their behavior AND acknowledge the deep pain we have felt, lived in and endured as a result of their drinking. But the sad truth is that's probably not going to happen. It's certainly not going to happen by virtue of them never taking another drink.

I feel as though it is redundant for me to repeatedly say alcoholism is complicated and complex but you know what? Alcoholism is complicated and complex and so the cure will, sadly, be equally so. It's not going to be a matter of getting the alcoholic to "just" stop drinking.

AA purports to be open to everyone, as is stated in Tradition Tree, "The only requirement for AA membership is a desire to stop drinking," but it's not open to everyone. It's open only to those who are willing to publicly declare themselves to be alcoholics or addicts and are willing to give up their inherent right of independence by declaring themselves powerless over addictive drugs and alcohol, as stated in Step One, "We admitted that we are powerless over alcohol - that our lives had become unmanageable."

Every person in the AA program who is successful is living proof that he or she does have power over addictive drugs or alcohol - the power to stop.

Chris Prentiss

The Alcoholism and Addiction Cure

SURIVIAL TIP #4

AA (Alcoholics Anonymous) Is The Answer.
AA Is Not The Answer

I'm not here to bash Alcoholics Anonymous though I am going to offer an alternative perspective on the AA institution. AA has done an amazing job - marketing geniuses really - at convincing the public that their way is The One and Only True Way to sobriety. The only problem is, like all marketing campaigns, their efforts are skewed to promote their own agenda.

Look, if someone finds their way out of the hell-hole of alcoholism through AA, I say great! Wonderful! Fantastic. Awesome. In fact, SPECTACULAR! Anything that releases another soul from the claws of this beast is to be applauded. Alcoholics Anonymous works. FOR SOME PEOPLE.

The truth is AA is just one recovery program. It is not the only program nor is it the perfect program. Like anything, it has its flaws and shortcomings. But most importantly, Alcoholics' Anonymous has no better recovery rate than any other program or approach. That's right. The sad truth is all recovery programs have pretty dismal success rates when it comes to the alcoholic achieving life-long, sustained sobriety.

I know when I was growing up and even well into my thirties, my understanding of alcoholism went something like this:

Alcoholics drank too much.

They needed to go to AA and never drink again.

If they wouldn't go to AA and never drink again, then they were no good drunks who wanted to remain no good drunks.

The End.

I didn't know that AA was a faith-based recovery program. (Which can be quite problematic - rightly so - for some people.)

I didn't know it was a "12-step" program, which again, is problematic for some.

I didn't know it required a near cult-like surrender to the doctrine.

I didn't even know it was controversial in the recovery community.

So why is AA so popular? Why does it enjoy a Sacred Cow-like status in our society at large?

First, it's free. You can't really beat free when it comes to anything - be it cookies or your alcoholism-recovery program.

Second, it's easy. Not easy as in easy to do or as in an easy way to recovery but easy as in easy to go to. (And easy for outsiders to decree it is what the alcoholic "needs.") To attend an AA meeting, all the alcoholic has to do is show up. Compared to finding a therapist or program, scheduling appointments and/or intake interviews, taking time off work or even a leave of absence, etc. etc., attending an AA meeting is easy. Imagine you are facing a court date for DUI? How opportune it is to say, "I started going to AA." It looks proactive but the truth is there is little requirement or accountability on the alcoholic's part. He doesn't have to actively participate in a meeting. He doesn't have to sign in. He doesn't have to pay! He just has to go. Once, twice...all his life or never again. Of course, no recovery program will ever work without the commitment of the patient but AA offers an extremely convenient way for the alcoholic to appear to be seeking recovery while avoiding any true accountability if he so chooses.

Additionally, Alcoholics Anonymous is shrouded in secrecy. In theory, the secrecy-part (i.e. anonymous) is meant to be a good thing. That's exactly how it is promoted by the AA brand. An individual can go to AA and no one will ever "out" him; no one will ever speak of it to him outside the meeting; no one will ever tell anyone they saw him there and no one will ever disclose anything he has said. When you are dealing with the historical shame of alcoholism along with the legalities and/or embarrassment of the alcoholic's behavior, anonymity is a much wanted, warranted and even justifiable requirement.

But because AA is so secret, most people don't really know what its doctrine or approach is. I would have continued forever in my ignorance as to the nature of AA had I not married an alcoholic. When you know nothing of alcoholism or recovery programs or even how rare and difficult recovery is, it's easy to believe a 12-step program can cure all.

And finally, I think one of the reasons AA enjoys a rather misplaced, hero-like standing in the community is that, whether purposely or not, it negates the medical emergency that alcoholism can become. My brother-in-law was a sad, tragic alcoholic, dead before 35 from the affliction. He was the kind of alcoholic who would have required medical intervention in order to detox. One evening a friend of his called, herself obviously an addict but nonetheless, her voice was filled with true concern for him. She was genuine and earnest but her hope, goal - main focus - was getting him to attend AA. I told her, as gently and best I could, that even if he would agree to go to AA, that was way (way, way, way, WAY!!) down the line. The most immediate and pressing need was getting him admitted to a hospital for a medically controlled detox. She couldn't hear what I was saying and clung to her hope that if only he would go to AA.

There comes a point in the alcoholic's drinking, when his body is so physically addicted to alcohol, that attending AA is, at the best, follow-up therapy. People die from alcohol withdraw.

DIE!

But you never hear of this in conjunction with the AA program and propaganda. Again, I don't know if it's by design or accidental but I believe AA is remiss in not acknowledging that it is not the program for every alcoholic. That be it personal beliefs, ideologies, personality or medical needs, individuals need to assess a recovery program from all angles to determine which program or platform will give them the best chance at success.

Here's a sad reality: most alcoholics do not seek recovery. However, just because your husband may refuse to go to Alcoholics Anonymous, it does not mean he wishes to remain a "no good drunk" or that he'll never seek treatment or that he can't be successful in a recovery program. It may just mean that even if he becomes willing to seek treatment, AA is not the program for him.

If there is one thing I learned in Al Anon, it's that you got to face the music because it grows louder when you ignore it.

Vickie Covington

Bird of Paradise

No one saves us but ourselves. No one can and no one may. We ourselves must walk the path.

Buddha

SURVIVAL TIP #5

AL-Anon Is The Answer. AL-Anon Is Not The Answer

Since I offered my own personal alternative perspective on Alcoholics Anonymous, I feel I'd be remiss if I didn't offer the same on its sister group, Al Anon. Al Anon is AA's answer to supporting the friends and families of alcoholics.

When I first, cautiously and tentatively, shared my husband's alcohol issues with a few trusted friends and family members, repeatedly I heard, "you need to go to Al-Anon." Much as the AA brand has successfully embedded itself in our society's collective psyche as the only game in town for obtaining sobriety, so has Al Anon taken up residency as the one and only, go-to answer for the friends and family members of alcoholics. I suspect many people who feel they are offering sage advice with the, "you need to go to Al-Anon" recommendation are not even fully aware of what the program is or the doctrine it follows.

But just as AA is - and is not - the answer, so is Al Anon the answer.

And not the answer.

I went to Al-Anon.

And for the first year I gained much from it. For starters, it was the first time I felt there was something I could actively DO. FOR ME! I no longer had to feel like a helpless, hapless victim at the mercy of my husband's drinking. And though I am vehemently opposed to the idea of "co-dependent," attending Al-Anon opened my eyes to how I was inadvertently engaging my husband when he was at his most hostile and combative.

The alcoholic needs justification for both his drinking and his behavior. One of his favorite, easiest ways of getting this is by drawing you, his wife, into his madness. He baits you. (See Tip #10). You, understandably, take it, and then he steps back, his beverage of choice in hand, and says "see why I drink?" The experiences and advice that others shared at Al-Anon were most beneficial in my learning to recognize this.

That being said, two things about Al-Anon are problematic for me. First, as I mentioned above, the philosophy of co-dependent and co-dependency is heavily supported. I, on the other hand, am staunchly not in support of what I call the accusation of co-dependency. The theory of co-dependency shifts the responsibility from the alcoholic to the wife and that is a responsibility I will never accept.

Second, the tenet behind Al-Anon is you need to "keep coming back." The program is predicated on the idea that you need to FOREVER attend Al-Anon. I don't think the goal of any sort of support – be it counseling, therapy, a group (even a book written by a "sister wife") - should be to create an eternal need in an individual. I think the purpose of such is to educate you, maybe offer some insight or enlightenment, help you grow as an individual and ultimately, set you free. I like to say Al-Anon helped me to unfurl my wings but I still had to teach myself how to fly with them.

So, go to Al-Anon if you like. Keep going if it fits you. But if it turns out to not be your thing, don't find fault in yourself, blame yourself or try to force yourself into it. Instead, look for the support, camaraderie, program and/or help that does resonate with you. After all, we have plenty of stress to endure on a daily basis as a result of being married to an alcoholic; the support we seek shouldn't add to it.

You can say sorry a million times, say I love you as much as you want, say whatever you want whenever you want. But if you're not going to prove these things you say are true, then don't say anything at all. Because if you can't show it, your words don't mean a thing.

Anonymous

SURVIVAL TIP #6

Beware The "Recovering" Alcoholic

Holy moly could I write forever on this. The "recovering" alcoholic (as in he's not really in recovery but he is choosing not to drink - temporarily) is a cunning creature! Let me say this: alcoholics tend to be very good studies of human nature. It's like they are fine-tuned into their wife's every feeling and emotion. They have to be: the alcoholic's wife is his support, his safety, his salvation. (Of course, in his mind she is also his damnation.) So, when you - the alcoholic's wife - are truly getting close to your breaking point, SOMEHOW YOUR ALCOHOLIC HUSBAND KNOWS THIS ON A SUBCONSCIOUS, CELLULAR SORT OF LEVEL. Like animals sensing an oncoming tsunami through a change in the atmospheric energy, the shift in your emotional and mental energy alerts your husband. But rather than retreating to higher ground, he retreats back to you. He pulls out all the stops. He stops drinking. He becomes present. Available. LOVING EVEN.

You can't believe it.

But you do. Foolishly. Hopefully. Perhaps even earnestly, depending on how many times you've been down this road.

BUT THE ALCOHOLIC CANNOT SUSTAIN THIS "NEW AND IMPROVED" VERSION OF HIMSELF, NO MATTER HOW MUCH HE FEARS LOSING YOU. EVENTUALLY (and usually a lot sooner than you would have preferred) HE WILL DRINK AGAIN.

This is the nature of alcoholism and being an alcoholic. (See Tip #1) So sadly, no matter how real his "recovery" may seem, and while probably the product of his very real fear of losing you, he can't sustain it. Not without real help. Professional help. Help that is beyond simply his effort at "white knuckling" it. So, don't be shocked. Don't be surprised. And, I'm sorry to say, don't be hopeful that his self-induced "recovery" is real.

One of the most important things to remember about alcoholism is its progression. Alcoholism begins in an early stage that looks nothing like a life-threatening illness, proceeds into a middle stage where problems begin to appear and intensify and gradually advances into the late, degenerative stage of obvious physiological dependence, physical and psychological deterioration and loss of control.

William F. Asbury

Beyond The Influence

First the man takes a drink; then the drink takes a drink; then the drink takes the man.

Japanese Proverb

SURVIVAL TIP #7

Know That He Will Get Worse. Alcoholism Is A Progressive Disorder/Disease

Not only can't the alcoholic spontaneously sober up on his own, the disease/disorder/condition is actually worsening every day, though on a daily basis you may not be aware of this. It's the old boiling-a-frog analogy. If you put a frog in boiling water, of course it will hop right out. But if you put it in cool water and slowly, gradually raise the temperature, the poor frog never realizes its pending fate. He sits as still and tranquil as if he were sunning himself on a lily pad while you get effortless – no need to chase an uncooperative frog around the kitchen – and delicious (delicious?) frog soup. As the wife of an alcoholic, I'm sorry to say my friend, you are the frog in a big ole pot and alcoholism is slowly, gradually but most certainly, turning up the heat.

Alcoholism IS (IS!!) a progressive disease. Not it can be. Not it is sometimes.

ALCOHOLISM IS ALWAYS PROGRESSIVE.

The alcoholic is systematically poisoning himself. He is literally damaging his brain day after day. And so when you read or hear stories about "end stage alcoholics" or you see women dealing with alcoholics who are "far worse" than yours, take heed. It's not that your alcoholic husband isn't that bad; it's he isn't that bad yet.

My husband didn't start out calling me a fucking bitch.

My husband didn't come into our marriage raging like a madman on fire because shoes were left in the bathroom.

We didn't always spend our days living together separately in our home.

38

Everything I am experiencing with him now - the verbal abuse, the anger, the disengagement from our relationship developed (or deteriorated if you like) over the course of nearly 20 years of marriage. If you are married to an alcoholic who is not "that bad" right now, he will be. One day. This isn't meant to scare you.

It's meant to warn you.

(And assure you that you are not crazy. Yes, he is getting worse. No, it wasn't always this bad.)

Your vision will become clear only when you look into your own heart. Who looks outside, dreams; who looks inside, awakens.

Carl Jung

SURVIVAL TIP #8

Know That The Alcoholic Projects His Worse Fears, His Greatest Self-Loathing And His Darkest Darkness Onto You, His Wife

My husband can speak to me with such contempt and loathing in his voice that I was once convinced that I must disgust him. Of course now I know far better; now I know that whatever anger and hatred he spews onto me is really a projection of the gravest thoughts and most haunting feelings he has about himself. But I didn't always know such.

Several years ago, back when I was young (in terms of dealing with an alcoholic husband anyway) and uninitiated in the ways of the alcoholic, we rented a beach house for our summer vacation. In planning for our trip, I came to suddenly (suddenly? finally!) notice that somewhere between having children, not losing the "baby weight" and managing life with an alcoholic husband, I had neglected my wardrobe. (And I use the word "wardrobe" loosely, very loosely.) In fact, I hadn't so much neglected it as completely abandoned it. Getting dressed meant nothing more than the logical issue of covering up my private bits. I lived in sweatpants and t-shirts. And not in that she's-so-adorable-and-sexy-in-sweats-and-a-raggy-t-shirt way of the movies! I looked dismal. I thought a t-shirt with long sleeves was "dressing up!" Getting dressed to go out somewhere meant, drum roll please, YOGA PANTS! Honestly, if I could have literally thrown a tent over my body, I probably would have. I doubt I could have looked much worse.

But this particular year of the beach house, for whatever unseen forces move us, I decided I would make a concerted effort to "dress cute" while on vacation. For starters, I willed myself to actually go shopping for clothes - not just grab something off the rack on my way through Target to

42

get milk and toilet paper. I went to a real live department store. And not just any department store.

I went to Nordstrom's! An expensive, well-lit, not a milk case or automotive aisle in sight, department store.

I'm sure I bought several pieces of clothing that day but what I remember most is a long, yellow, gauzy, Bohemian-ish skirt. I was totally outside my comfort zone buying it but I told myself had I seen another woman wearing it, I would have thought it soooooooo cute!

I donned it eagerly the first day of our vacation and set out for an early morning walk on the beach. I mean doesn't the image just sound cute? Walking on the beach, barefoot naturally, wearing a yellow, hippy-dippy skirt. I bet the surf even wetted the hem ever so perfectly.

And when I returned to our beach house, my husband took me in his arms, gave me a big kiss and said, "there's my beautiful bride." Oh wait, I think that line is meant for a piece of fiction I am working on.

No, when I returned to our rental house my husband laid into me for "letting" our kids get paint on the patio table.

"YOU LET THE KIDS GET PAINT ALL OVER THIS TABLE! WE ARE NEVER GETTING OUR SECURITY DEPOSIT BACK!" He screamed, violently scrubbing the table as if he were prepping it for an emergency heart transplant.

Now never mind that it was water based, kid paint. And never mind that in all the years of renting vacation homes, we have always gotten our security deposit back. Never mind even that he was screaming at his wife over kiddie paint while on vacation at the beach. He could have tried, you know, just talking to me about it.

I tried to assure him that the water-based, kids-could-drink-it-it's-so-benign, paint would indeed come off the glass patio table. But he was having none of that. Why listen to reason when you have found something to justify your rage and anger? The argument quickly degenerated into a yelling match about a host of unrelated and random topics - as is the usual case when trying to argue or discuss or resolve anything with an alcoholic - when he shouted at me,

"AND JUST LOOK AT YOURSELF!"

I demanded to know what he meant by that but he refused to explain himself. And while I now know, in the most definitive of ways, that he didn't explain himself because he couldn't, because what he really meant was, "just look at me! Look at what I am becoming!" I had none of that awareness back then. Instead I mistakenly, sadly, heartbreakingly allowed him to project his darkness onto me, which I in turn internalized. Took as the truth.

Made it my own.

It may seem silly - though it's really more tragic - but I was convinced his accusation had everything to do with how ridiculous, fat and frumpy I looked in my long, gauzy Bohemian skirt. It breaks my heart to think of how attacked and vulnerable I felt in that moment.

I can't say exactly how the argument ended or when I took the skirt off. I know I didn't run from the room wailing, ripping the skirt off and flinging it down the stairs with a dramatic flair that could rival Scarlet O'Hara. I do know I took it off. That day. And never wore it again. In fact, it ended up in the Goodwill bag once we returned home. It killed me to give it away - it certainly wasn't cheap, but I knew I would never, ever, EVER wear it again, so haunting (and effective) were my husband's words.

Of course, the truth is I could have looked like an elephant in a tutu and still my husband's words would have had nothing - nothing, nothing, NOTHING - to do with me. Whatever - WHATEVER - your husband says to you that is cruel and cutting, no matter HOW "accurate" or "applicable" it seems to you, it is always - always, ALWAYS - a projection of his darkness onto your light. In fact, the more applicable or justifiable you feel your husband's words to be, the more assured you can be that this is his way of dumping his ugliness onto your back.

44

Why? Because the alcoholic husband aligns his self-hatred with your insecurities. I know it sounds crazy (and like a lot of mental work but trust me, it comes naturally to the alcoholic) but it's what the alcoholic does. If you feel uncomfortable about how you look, he ridicules your appearance though it's really his own appearance that he's unhappy with or ashamed of. If everyone around you went to college and he knows you feel insecure about that, you can bet he will pull that arrow out of his alcoholic quiver and yet, make no mistake; his painful, harsh words about *your* intelligence, *your* education, even your *innate* worth are all really about himself. For Pete's sake, a woman could be insecure about her cookware and you can bet her alcoholic husband would find a way to ridicule her and make her feel *even worse* about it.

How, you ask. As in how can our alcoholic husbands be SO cruel to us, their wives?

Sadly, the answer is... easy. As in, it is easy for the alcoholic to be so cruel and hateful toward his wife. The alcoholic knows. He KNOWS he is an alcoholic. (See Tip #9) He knows he is messing up. He knows his behavior is disgusting and dismal. He knows he would lose everything if he lost you. But all that fear, all that self-hatred is far, far too powerful and painful for him to handle or process within himself. So he spews it onto the closest, safest person.

Yep, his wife.

Remember this:

EVERY SINGLE VICIOUS WORD, PHRASE, ACCUSATION OR "ASSESSMENT" OF YOU BY YOUR ALCOHOLIC HUSBAND IS REALLY A PROJECTION ONTO YOU OF THE TRUE AND TRAGIC FEELINGS HE HOLDS ABOUT HIMSELF.

The self-loathing your husband carries within himself is a heavy, heavy burden and eventually he has to set it down somewhere. That somewhere is you. It never gets easy being called a fucking bitch, whore, cunt or whatever. It never stops hurting to be told you're a horrible mother, wife, lover. But it can help you maintain your sense of self and innate value

45

as a human being if you work hard at remembering this: his words, his feelings, his disappointment and his disgust are actually meant for himself. Everything - and I mean EVERYTHING - he says about you or accuses you of or claims are your shortcomings, is really (really!) about himself.

Even if you look like an elephant in a tutu.

Drugs and alcohol are not my problem, reality is my problem, drugs and alcohol my solution.

Russell Brand

The Alcoholic Knows He Has A Drinking Problem

I know the AA model has done a good job of perpetuating the myth that the alcoholic is in such deep denial that he doesn't "know" he has a problem.

He knows.

Of course he knows.

That's why he's so mean and angry and hostile.

He's lost control of himself and his life to the bottle.

The denial part comes in terms of minimizing (or denying. Hence the term...) the extent of his problem and the MAGNITUDE TO WHICH HIS DRINKING IS AFFECTING THOSE AROUND HIM.

"You're over-reacting."

"You're just a bitch."

"Everyone gets drunk on the weekends."

"I don't drink that much."

"I don't have to drink."

"I can stop drinking anytime I want to. I just don't want to."

That's one of my favorites.

"I can stop if I wanted to but I don't want to."

Really? He doesn't WANT to stop doing something that is literally killing him, making everyone around him miserable and destroying his family life?

Etc., etc., etc. Blah, blah, blah, blah, blah!

When the alcoholic lays his head down at night - or wakes up with yet another hangover from hell; when he calls in sick again; when he can't get out of bed all day; when he's screaming at his wife that she's a fucking bitch or telling the kids to let the fucking dog out, don't for one minute think he really believes he's just a little "under the weather" or it's no big deal or he's not that bad.

He knows.

He knows it's that bad and it's a big deal and he's in deep trouble.

Yep, he knows.

And he's so scared that he is paralyzed by his own fear. Paralyzed in a Greek tragedy sort of way because the only thing he knows to do - the only way he knows to "fix" whatever is wrong in his life - is to drink.

And deny.

THE COCK AND THE FOX

One bright evening as the sun was sinking on a glorious world a wise old cock flew into a tree to roost. Before he composed himself to rest, he flapped his wings three times and crowed loudly. Just as he was about to put his head under his wing, his beady eyes caught a flash on red and a glimpse of a long-pointed nose and there just below him stood Mister Fox.

"Have you heard the wonderful news?" cried the Fox in a very joyful and excited manner.

"What news," asked the Cock calmly. But he had a queer, fluttery feeling inside him, for, you know, he was very much afraid of the fox.

"Your family and mine and all other animals have agreed to forget their differences and live in peace and friendship from now on forever. Just think of it! I simply cannot wait to embrace you! Do come down dear friend and let us celebrate the joyful event."

"How grand," said the Cock. "I certainly am delighted at the news." But he spoke in an absent way, and stretching up on tiptoes, seemed to be looking at something far off.

"What is it you see?" asked the Fox a little anxiously.

"Why, it looks to me like a couple of Dogs coming this way. They must have heard the good news as well."

But the Fox did not wait to hear more. Off he started in a run.

"Wait," cried the Cock. "Why do you run? The Dogs are friends of yours now."

"Yes," answered the Fox, "but they might not have heard the news. Besides, I have a very important errand that I almost forgot about."

The Cock smiled as he buried his head in his feathers and went to sleep, for he had succeeded in outwitting a very crafty enemy.

An Aesop Fable

SURVIVAL TIP #10

Learn How To Recognize When Your Husband Is Baiting You – And How to Not Take it!

I will admit when I first went to Al Anon, I was quite defensive in my stand that I was neither an enabler nor co-dependent. And it's true, I'm not! You probably aren't either - even if you do bring a bottle of wine or six pack of beer into your house. You and I are mature adults who can HANDLE alcohol. Perhaps we would like to have the occasional glass of wine or beer in the comfort of our own homes. I do not "depend" on my husband to drink and I do not "enable" him just because I don't (TRY!) to stop him. (See Survival Tip #11)

So yes, initially anyway, I was a little resistant to the idea that I could in anyway be responsible for things escalating between me and my alcoholic husband. I certainly didn't - still don't - believe I was or am responsible for his behavior. However, what I did learn at Al Anon is that while I am not responsible for my husband's drinking or his behavior, the way I react to him in any given situation can greatly impact how I feel both about him and about myself in any given situation. I will concede that those early Al Anon meetings showed me that I was most certainly not setting boundaries with my husband.

In fact, 99 times out of 100, I was taking his bait.

Remember, the alcoholic needs you to fight with him. That's right, he NEEDS you to fight. For it is in your fighting with him that he gets to justify his drinking.

"See," the demented logic plays in his head, "she is always nagging me about leaving my dirty clothes on the floor. I can't do anything right. She is never happy. Why do I even try?" Etc., etc., ETC! He will convince himself that because of you, he has to drink. "I didn't even want a beer/gin and tonic/straight vodka before I got home tonight but she makes me drink."

Yes, the loop in his head really sounds something like that! Consequently, your husband is always on the lookout for an excuse to drink. And ironically the more you resist, the more he will keep looking and pushing and baiting you to give him said excuses.

I USE TO FALL FOR IT EVERY! SINGLE! TIME!

My husband would say something ridiculous or respond to something I said with the most absurd answer and I would chomp down on the bait like a Muskie in Minnesota. (We use to fish there when I was a kid: The Muskie is a very aggressive fish!) Next thing you know, we're yelling and screaming at each other and he's got his "get out of jail free" card (i.e. "drink all you want free" card). But after a few months at Al Anon, I began to notice HIS pattern.

For example, one night he was cooking mini pizzas in the oven while I was waiting to use the oven to bake cookies. I needed to turn the oven temperature down from where he had it set. He told me he would tell me when he was finished.

I saw him eat two small pizzas - his usual pizza quota - and assumed he had forgotten to tell me he was done with the oven. (He's been known to leave the oven on once he's finished with it. Ok, he always leaves the oven on once he's finished with it). I turned the temperature from 400 to 350 without realizing he actually had two more pizzas in there.

"WHY'D YOU TURN DOWN THE OVEN?!" He bellowed upon discovering my most grievous error.

"I thought you were done."

"I TOLD YOU I'D TELL YOU WHEN I WAS DONE!!"

Now here's the point where I would usually snap but instead I calmly said, "Oh, I'm sorry. I didn't know you were having more than two pizzas."

"WHAT DIFFERENCE DOES THAT MAKE?!!"

See what he is doing there? He's not accepting my apology or conceding how it could be understandable that I made a simple mistake.

"It doesn't," I remained calm, "I was just explaining why I thought I could use the oven."

"I DON'T KNOW WHY YOU HAD TO TURN THE OVEN DOWN WHEN I TOLD YOU I'D TELL YOU WHEN I WAS DONE!"

See there, still more posturing. Still dangling that bait in front of me.

"I was mistaken. I'm sorry…"

"WHATEVER!"

But then he huffed off because even an alcoholic knows when he's been bested.

Similarly, arguments would erupt between us when we were on the phone with one another. He'd call me a fucking bitch and/or an assorted sundry of other equally lovely names. I would declare to him that he CANNOT talk to me like that and hang up.

ONLY TO CALL HIM RIGHT BACK!

Yes, I would call him back and demand he talked to me "better."

Huh?

Of course, he didn't talk to me any "better."   Why would he? I'd already demonstrated that I was willing to pony up to his bar of abuse for another. But even more critical is the fact that he needed the fighting to continue so he would feel justify in popping open a beer (or eight) when he got home.

The alcoholic wants to argue.

He wants to argue. He wants to argue. He. Wants. To. Argue.

Not because he is right.

Not because he thinks anything will be resolved.

Not even because he loves the great makeup sex you two have afterwards.

He wants to argue so he can feel less like an ass when he gets tanked (again). He wants to argue so he doesn't have to face his own demons. He wants to argue so the beer or wine or vodka or whiskey or gin or rum (or all of them?) tastes like warranted compensation. Not your bitter tears.

So remember, if your alcoholic husband is saying something particularly inflammatory, absurd, ridiculous or unreasonable, chances are pretty good that's exactly his intention! He's trying to draw you into a fight so that he can justify his own behavior.

Don't take the bait.

I've lived with many alcoholic men over the years and each one has taught me that it is useless to worry, fruitless to ask why, suicide to try to help them. They are who they are for better and worse.

Ottessa Moshfegh

"Eileen"

SURVIVAL TIP #11

Do Yourself A Favor And Don't Look For -- Or Throw Out – His Stash Of Alcohol. And Don't Waste Your Time Or Good Energy Arguing With Him About His Drinking Either!

In the early years of our marriage/his drinking, my husband never really hid his beer from me. He just didn't leave it sitting out in the open. That didn't stop me though from going on the occasional scavenger hunt in search of his stash. I'm not sure why I went looking for it; it never required much "scavenging." In the summer time it was in his shop; in the winter, he stuck it outside the backdoor, taking advantage of nature's natural refrigeration. Sadly, there is a photograph of my son, age three, running out the backdoor and through the snow in just his underwear. With a case of Bud Light in the background, sitting in the snow outside the back door.

I had taken the photo because I wanted to capture my three-year-old running out the back door and through the snow in just his underwear. I never noticed the beer. Years later when I happened upon the picture, I saw I had captured far more about our lives than I realized.

I don't know why I looked for his beer. I knew it was there. To find it wasn't to find out anything I didn't already know. Maybe it's a rite of passage for all women who are married to alcoholics.

Luckily, I understood quite quickly that I didn't want to spend my life foraging for what I never really wanted to find anyway. Let me be really clear and blunt about this:

THERE IS ABSOLUTELY, POSITIVELY NO (NONE, NADA, ZIP, ZIPPO) REASON TO LOOK FOR HIS ALCOHOL. EVEN IF HE HIDES IT LIKE A SQUIRREL

HIDING WINTER NUTS! NOTHING - AND I MEAN NOTHING! - WILL COME OF IT.

First of all, you already know (know, know…KNOW) it's there, so what are you really looking for? Confirmation of something you already know is confirmed? There's nothing to be gained by searching for it and much to be lost - mainly your self-respect. It's degrading and demoralizing to be pulling open drawers, overturning trash cans and digging under boxes to find what you don't even want to find in the first place. When I did look around the house for my husband's beer, it hurt my soul! I felt embarrassed and belittled even though there was no one around for me to be embarrassed or belittled in front of. Myself I guess.

Don't do it.

It's humiliating.

But know what? You are probably going to do it. Initially anyway. But, in the interim, while you are feeling you just *have* to search for his booze, at least heed this suggestion:

Don't throw it out.

You know why?

Ok, this might sound shocking but…

He'll…

Just….

Buy….

MORE!

It's really that simple. Prohibition didn't stop human begins from drinking. Closing the liquor stores on Sundays doesn't stop anyone. And you pouring a few fifths down the drain or tossing a case or two of beer in the trash is certainly not going to stop your alcoholic husband from drinking compulsively.

Protect your time, dignity and frankly, bank account.

As for arguing with him over his drinking, to un-paraphrase the Nike ad, Just DON'T Do It. I know it can seem as though you have a completely logical, perfectly reasonable argument to make. I'm sure you do. But there is NOTHING logical - completely or otherwise - or perfectly reasonable about alcoholism and the alcoholic.

You can talk about his health. You can talk about the children. You can point out the jobs he's lost or the job he is about to lose. You can threaten divorce. You can threaten the police. You could build a bonfire with the over-due notices for bills that are piling up. You can produce a dumpster full of "empties" from his last bender.

You could put on a song and dance show, that rivals the grandest Broadway musical, about the ills of his drinking.

And it all would still fall flat upon deaf (drunk) ears.

THERE IS NOTHING YOU CAN SAY; NO ARGUMENT YOU CAN MAKE; NO EVIDENCE YOU CAN PRODUCE; NO FACTS YOU CAN EXTOL UPON THE ALCOHOLIC THAT WILL MAKE HIM CONCEDE OR ADMIT HE HAS A DRINKING PROBLEM!!

AND THERE IS REALLY, REALLY, REALLY (!!!!) NOTHING YOU CAN SAY TO MAKE HIM STOP DRINKING.

YOU CAN'T ARGUE AN ALCOHOLIC INTO SOBRIETY. (See Tip #1)

When you are living with an alcoholic, there comes a point where you have to consider your actions and choices from the point of view of how it helps or hurts you. Arguing with your alcoholic husband about his compulsive drinking and/or trying to convince him to seek help or treatment only comes to drain and deplete you. While not making so much as a tiny dent in his alcoholic armor.

With some people we may have a history of good times, we feel invested in the relationship, and we keep thinking (hoping) if we stick around long enough the other person will "break down" and give us what we think we need. Write this on the palm of your hand if you need to: No one can give you what they do not have. Simplistic example: You come to my door needing to borrow a welding torch. I don't own a welding torch. No matter how much I want to lend you one, I don't have one to lend you....

Christopher Kennedy Lawford

What Addicts Know

SURVIVAL TIP #12

Come To Expect Nothing Of -- Or From --
The Alcoholic

This is not only one of the most important and necessary survival tools, it's one of THE HARDEST things to learn to do and incorporate into your daily living. Indeed, it will probably always be more of a continued work in progress than a completed task. I know I still have to make a conscious effort to remember every single day: expect nothing.

It sounds simple enough.

Expect nothing.

Except your heart and head will be screaming (rightfully so),

EXEPCT NOTHING? How am I supposed to expect NOTHING of an individual? And not just any individual, but my husband? The man I chose to spend my life. How am I supposed to expect nothing from the one person who is supposed to be there for me for everything?"

Well, it's certainly not easy. Not easy at all. And what makes it even more maddening and frustrating is that it gets harder – not easier! - the more you practice it. Things are supposed to get easier the more you do them, right? Going for that morning walk, refraining from a daily McDonald's sausage egg and cheese biscuit, riding a bike. All these things got (or would get) easier if and when we practiced them. But expecting nothing of our alcoholic husbands? Numbing your heart to yet another let down, another disappointment? That doesn't get easier.

It gets harder!

The alcoholic's wife starts out her marriage like any other wife: expectant of love, support, communication, camaraderie, emotional presence, kindness and yes, even conflict resolution. And it's not to say we demand perfection or think of ourselves as perfect. I don't know any alcoholic's wife that ever said, "I thought marriage would be perfect. I thought we'd never argue or have disagreements. I thought he'd read my mind, fulfil my every need and never fail to instinctively know what I want and need." No, it's not that we expected marriages out of a Disney movie; it's just we expected...marriage. You know, where two people are a team, "in this together," communicating, fighting, loving, arguing, compromising, supporting, dreaming...Living and sharing life TOGETHER! In other words, the basic premise of being married.

As our marriages (and his alcoholism) progress, we start to become aware that there really is no support or communication, no camaraderie, emotional presence, kindness or even conflict resolution. There is just expectations and disappointment. So, like some sort of emotional natural selection - and perhaps without us even being aware of it - we start to dumb down what we expect. We stop telling our husbands "pointless" little stories about our day; we stop sharing our fears, our hopes, our dreams. We stop talking about the kids, planning for the future or even mentioning toilet paper is on sale at the local supermarket. Bit by bit we withdraw, asking and expecting less and less.

And the less we expect, the more we expect of the little we do expect. (If you understand that perfectly, you're definitely married to an alcoholic.) Again, the less we expect, the more we expect of the little we do expect.

We cling to the idea that if we only expect the minimum then we can hold out hope for some semblance of a "normal" marriage and family.

And that's where we get in trouble.

Because we have so minimized our expectations of our husbands, it's as if we get even angrier when they fail to meet these minimums. It's like we say to ourselves, "Ok, we're never going to talk about anything deep; we're never going to dream and plan our futures together; he's never going to support or encourage me in my life but can't he JUST CLOSE THE FLIPPIN'

KITCHEN CABINETS! CAN'T HE CLEAN THE KITCHEN WHEN I'M AWAY ATTENDING A FAMILY FUNERAL?! CAN'T HE PUT THE TOILET PAPER ON THE ROLL?

CAN'T HE REMEMBER I WAS CALLING THE DOCTOR ABOUT MY MAMMOGRAM RESULTS THAT HE THOUGHT LOOKED "SUSPICIOUS?"

No, no he can't.

As shocking and unbelievable as this sounds, even the most basic or minimal of expectations for his role in your marriage are often too much for the alcoholic.

And beyond what he has to give.

I use to try - GOD I TRIED! - to communicate with my husband and actually resolve an issue or argument. I would tread Oh! So! Carefully! I would use all those phrases you are supposed to use, like "this makes me feel," and "I fee." I tried to always be mindful of not sounding like I was blaming or attacking him.

IT DID NO GOOD!

You know what he told me once?

He said, "You think you can just put "this makes me feel..." in front of anything you want to say and that makes it ok to say."

Over and over, again and again through the years I would go to him, determined to have a productive but kind and mutually respectfully discussion with him. And over and over, again and again through the years it ended in verbal bloodshed.

The alcoholic can't give WHAT HE DOESN'T HAVE! And while that concept is easy to grasp and understand, it's not easy to grasp and understand how it is he doesn't have the most basic of interpersonal relationship skills.

I don't know how he doesn't but I do know this:

HE DOESN'T!

He can't put your needs before his. He can't put the needs of your children or the family's or even the marriage's before his. He can't go outside himself, so to speak, and say, "hmm, how is this making her feel? What is this doing to my marriage? Why wouldn't I do this for my wife?"

I use to have a part-time job literally minutes from our house. One evening I called my husband and asked if he would run up with some food for me for dinner. His exact answer, verbatim, was, "I don't want to."

I hung up the phone, mortified in front of my co-workers. They may not have heard my husband's exact words but his sentiment was obvious. All the years of being called a "fucking bitch" or told to "shut the fuck up," you would think not much could make me cry anymore. And yet, there I was, trying to stall the tears that were welling up in my eyes. Later, when I asked my husband why he wouldn't just bring me some leftovers, his response was,

"Oh, I thought you wanted me to go somewhere and get you food."

Why yes, I actually expected him to fly to France and get me some truffles. Or maybe drive to Philadelphia for a world-famous Philly-cheese steak." Naturally, I wanted to scream, "WHAT DIFFERENCE WOULD THAT HAVE MADE?!"

It made complete sense to him that since he erroneously believed my request would have required him to have to actually go somewhere - like the McDonald's drive thru - to get the food, his response was valid.

Again, I don't know how it is they don't have it to give but THEY DON'T! And it doesn't matter how little you expect of them. It doesn't matter how low you lower your expectations. Our (rational) minds want to believe something like this;

"All I expect is for you to pick up after yourself. And not call me a fucking bitch. And maybe look at me and acknowledge what I am saying when I am trying to talk to you. So, since that is all I am expecting..."

That makes sense to you. It makes sense to me. It does not make sense to your alcoholic husband. In fact, it's beyond what he is even capable of processing. The alcoholic husband doesn't walk around saying,

"Well I'm not going to give to my wife. I'm not going to be present and emotionally available in this marriage."

Worse than that.

You're not really on his radar.

Not really.

You, your needs, the marriage, the needs of the marriage are all secondary to his mistress – alcohol.

So save yourself a lot of (additional) pain and come to terms with the fact that your husband can't give what he doesn't even know he doesn't have to give.

Why do you stay in prison? When the door is so wide open.

Rumi

Sometimes you must seem to hurt something in order to do good for it.

Susan Cooper

The Grey King

On any given day it was easier for her to stay; in the long run, it would have been easier for her to leave.

A friend, assessing how it

was his mother remained married

to his alcoholic father for over 35 years

SURVIVAL TIP #13

Leaving Isn't Always The Answer. One Day Leaving Will Be The Only Answer

Had I not married an alcoholic myself, I may have well gone my entire life believing the "solution" to an alcoholic marriage was divorce. I would have been one of those (self-righteous?) people wondering how on Earth it is that any woman stays married to a "no good drunk" one minute longer than necessary. But alas, I did marry an alcoholic and so I know the leave/stay question is hardly that simple. In fact, I have become quite protective and defensive of women's choices to stay with their alcoholic husbands. Hell, as I write this my own alcoholic husband is home asleep, no doubt planning a trip to the beer store later today on what could be a lovely, family-centered Sunday afternoon. So it's not as though I don't know the struggle, the conflict, the internal battle raging in the wives of alcoholics regarding the Leaving Issue. People who want to offer the astute advice of "leave the bastard," "send the bum packing," and the ever helpful, "kick his ass to the curb," are, to be rather un-literary, clueless. They are predicating such "advice" on a) the idea that the Leaving Issue is a stagnant decision that the alcoholic's wife simply makes once and is done with it and b) the ILLUSION that all will be solved for the alcoholic's wife simply by removing the alcoholic from her home and marriage.

No one thinks about leaving the alcoholic husband more than his wife! It's a question we weigh, contemplate, fear and long for a definitive answer to on a near daily basis. But it's not a stagnant decision. It's not something we can contemplate on a linear plane and finally arrive at The Final Decision. We are married. And albeit while that marriage is to an alcoholic, it doesn't mean the entanglement of our two lives are any less than in a healthy marriage.

First up, front and center is the most obvious: financial. Most women are not in the financial position to leave or "kick" their alcoholic husbands "to the curb." Myself, I have been home with my kids since they were born. I home school them. If I wanted to leave my husband at this point in our lives, the degree of changes my children would have to endure would be far more traumatic than me staying in the marriage. I would have to go back to work full time. The kids would have to leave their home school friends and community and go to "regular" school. They would have to bear the dissolution of their home, their parents' marriage, and the life they have always lived. For my children it is better, for now anyway, that I stay in the marriage. And while it's not simple for me, it's really that simple when it comes to what is best for my children.

It's not that I, or any wife of an alcoholic who has children, thinks home life with an alcoholic father is a grand situation for our children to be in. We wonder and worry about what our children are absorbing in terms of how relationships and marriages work, how fathers treat their children and how husbands treat their wives. We worry about how the daily stress of living in an alcoholic household is affecting them. We fear their exposure to the compulsive drinking. What attitudes and beliefs are they internalizing about alcohol and alcohol abuse? When you are in an alcoholic marriage with children, it is often a choice between the "devil and the deep blue sea." No choice is ideal or even preferable. For me, right now, the devil seems more manageable than the deep blue sea.

But even if a woman doesn't have children, it doesn't mean the leaving-answer is any simpler or more straight forward. Some women stay because they have pets they can't bear to give up. Some stay because they have perennial gardens and dream cottages they have spent years cultivating and decorating. Some stay because they still feel young enough to bear it; some stay because they feel too old to leave. The point is women stay for A LOT of different reasons and usually the reasons are tangled up with one another like a clump of necklaces found in the bottom of a jewelry box. Why do women stay? I think ultimately it comes down to one factor and one factor only:

Life with the alcoholic husband is EASIER to manage IN the marriage than OUT of the marriage.

Until one day when it won't be.

Until one day the problems you will encounter by leaving are more manageable than the problems you are managing by staying.

Yes, I know I just said leaving isn't necessarily the answer and it doesn't necessarily fix anything but you still need to leave. Or at least prepare to.

Just as I predicted when I sat down this morning to start writing, my husband has spent the day drinking beer and watching television and yet, I'm not anticipating leaving anytime soon. Financially I can't and quite frankly, emotionally I not quite ready either. I am not saying or advocating or proclaiming you have to leave NOW. What I am saying, advocating and proclaiming, is that you need to prepare to leave now so if and when you want to leave later, you can. If your boat isn't seaworthy, do you prep and prepare it before you go to sea or do you wait until you're at sea and water is flooding in?

Exactly.

Waiting until you are drowning in your life with an alcoholic husband before preparing yourself to leave is like voyaging out into the ocean on a boat with a hull full of holes - and then trying to repair it.

Maybe it won't come down to you leaving.

Maybe your husband will seek help and gain true sobriety.

Maybe pigs will fly by my window any minute.

Regardless, you really (really, really, REALLY) want to start putting into place a "use in case of emergency" exit plan. The tragic paradox of being married to an alcoholic is that when you have the emotional, spiritual and mental energy to potentially leave, you don't yet feel the need.

And when you finally feel the need?

Yep, you guessed it. Your emotional, spiritual and mental energy will be depleted to the extent that you feel powerless, helpless, overwhelmed and defeated.

Life draws from one source - our souls - and when there is nothing left, there is nothing left. The alcoholic and his companion Alcoholism are eating away at your very being little by little Every. Single. Day. So you can't wait until you have realized you are nearly devoured to say, "Wow, I guess I better start planning something now." It doesn't have to be an all-encompassing plan. You don't need to implement it immediately. But you do need to start. You do need to lay a few bricks every day. If you are a stay-at-home mom, think about what you love to do and/or have a talent for. Start pursuing your hobbies or that one thing you "always wanted to do." Maybe you can get a part-time job. I got a part-time job for just ten hours a week, at only $8.50 an hour but the sense of empowerment was far greater than my hourly wage! If you work already, is it something that can support you and your children without your husband's income? Are there classes or training you can do? Do you want to jump careers or industries all together?

The main point is START. PLANNING. TO LEAVE. NOW.

Before you are ready.

Because if you don't start before you are ready, there's a good chance you won't be able to when you are.

Most of us GREATLY underestimate the power of small actions. We look at our actions in terms of what we will get LITERALLY and IMMEDIATELY without realizing that the real power in our actions - no matter how small or seemingly insignificant - is the movement they create in our lives and within ourselves. As the saying goes, "an object in motion will stay in motion." When you are married to an alcoholic, it feels as if you gravitate, without even being aware of it, to an opposite state: an object not in motion stays not in motion. We become stuck. Trapped. Immovable. There seems to be SO MUCH to do and fix in regards to our marriage, ourselves, our kids, and our lives, that we become paralyzed. Doing little things, taking small steps every single day will create a shift within you as well as prepare your life so that if or when you want to leave, you can.

What do you do when the one person you want comfort from the most is the one who caused your pain? How can I want so desperately for him to wrap me up in his arms but also want so much for him to leave me alone?

Amanda Grace

But I Love Him

SURVIVAL TIP #14

It's Highly Unlikely Your Alcoholic Husband Will Ever Voluntarily Leave You

If you are relatively new to this alcoholic husband thing, I suspect your husband threatens you, on some sort of regular basis, to leave or divorce you. And you, new to the idle threats of the alcoholic husband, may actually fear he will. Let me put your mind as ease: your alcoholic husband is not leaving you.

No matter how much he claims you are the evilest, wickedest bitch to ever grace the Earth; no matter how often he tells you his life would be so much better without you; even if he brags he could get someone "new" "tomorrow," he's NOT going ANYWHERE.

You provide the physical and emotional base from which he can live his life. You close the kitchen cabinet doors. You feed the cat, take the dog to the vet and get the kids to swim/baseball/soccer practice. You do the laundry, clean the lint trap, wipe up food spills in the refrigerator and clean the sticky stuff off the floor. You don't do this because you are an "enabler" or "co-dependent." You do this because you are a wife - his wife - and that's what wives do. They create homes. What are you supposed to do? Leave yourself and your children to live in physical squalor so that he might not "benefit." It's enough to survive the emotional squalor of living with an alcoholic.

And he knows this! On some subconscious, cellular, metaphysical level, he knows that you can't not do for him because it would result in your not doing for the entire family.

But it's not just getting Fido to the vet or picking up his dirty socks from in front of the television that keeps him warm and safe in life. You also provide the emotional base and outlet for his life. You shoulder all his self-loathing and hatred. All his anger, rage and denial. You stand strong and stoic like a gladiator in the arena as he pounds you with all that threatens to consume him.

He knows he can't survive without you.

HE KNOWS.

And ironically, tragically, this only serves to intensify his fury against you.

No, your alcoholic husband is not going anywhere. And while at first you fear he'll carry out on his threats to leave you, sadly, one day you may come to fear that he won't.

*The one caveat to an alcoholic not leaving his wife is if - if, if, IF - he finds a new woman to take him in. But even then, there's a good chance he'll be back. (Maybe even quicker than you would like.) I say this with all sincerity, it takes a special woman to bear the alcoholic's burden and chances are he's not going to find that (not easily anyway) in someone other than you.

I was out of my marriage. I had "kicked the bum to the curb," as so many had advised me, even admonished me to do. Then one day he came back and said, "Either take me back or I will move in with our daughter." What was I to do? My daughter had her own child to raise, her own life to live. She hadn't taken a vow to him "for better or worse." I did the only thing I felt I could do as a mother. When he first moved back in, he continued to drink and deteriorate but he also continued to defy the odds. By all rights, he should have been dead a long time ago. But instead, he just kept getting sicker and sicker. Until one day, for me anyway, there was a shift and it was no longer about being a mother or a wife. It was about being a moral human being. This was a very sick man and yes, he had brought it all on with his choice to drink but again, what could I do? He was still a human being. And to turn him out would have meant sending him to literally die in the street.

Linda Doyne

Author and Blogger, The ImmortalAlcoholic.blogspot.com

SURVIVAL TIP #15

There Is A Point Of No Return

I believe every woman married to or in a serious relationship with an alcoholic needs to make the choices and decisions that fit her life and her situation but let me just say this:

IF YOU ARE IN A MARRIAGE OR RELATIONSHIP WITH AN ALCOHOLIC AND YOU DO NOT HAVE CHILDREN TOGETHER:

RUN!

I'm sorry but RUN! Run far, far away. RUN NOW! STOP READING THIS BOOK AND RUN! GO ON! JUST DROP IT WHERE YOU ARE AND RUNNY, RUN, RUN! WHY ARE YOU STILL HERE?! WHY AREN'T YOU RUNNING AWAY?!

Ok, but seriously (well seriously RUN but anyway...) if you are in a young or new relationship and/or you don't have children together, I'd start packing.

IT'S NOT WORTH IT! BELIEVE ME.

With that said, I will say there is a point of no return.

Just ask my friend Linda who writes the blog TheImmortalAlcoholic.blogspot.com. She has far more experience with alcoholics - particularly end stage alcoholics - than she ever dreamed or expected she'd have, that's for sure. Her story in a very small nutshell:

She left her alcoholic husband. Bye bye.

Kicked the bastard to the curb, as they like to tell us to do.

Adios.

Off the mortgage.

Out of her bank account.

Gone, bye bye, no more marriage.

As I write this, she is going on ten years of caring for her end-stage, was-to-be-her-ex, alcoholic husband. What happened you ask?

He continued to drink. Linda "kicking his ass to the curb" did nothing to deter this. He got sicker and sicker as his alcoholism progressed and then one day he appeared on her doorstep and said,

"Take me back (and care for me though he never actually said that) or I'll move in with our daughter."

Well if that isn't the ultimate trump card.

I will tell you, Linda has received a lot of criticism for taking him back rather than letting him follow through with what was most certainly NOT an idle threat. I though agree 110 zillion kazillion percent with Linda's choice. If it came down to a choice between me and my life or my children, their lives and their families, hands down I would not let that happen to them.

So that was Linda's point of no return. Your point of no return could be the same or it could be different. It could be dictated by morals or finances or other circumstances in your life that are beyond your control. (And that you possibly can't even fathom right now.) So I'm not saying leave TODAY; I'm not saying kick him out TOMORROW.

I'm just saying there will come a day when leaving is no longer an option. When the sense of choice you have now - even if it seems a very difficult choice to make - is no more. There is a wolf at your door and its name is Alcoholism. Sooner or later, one way or another, he IS getting in. Heck, he's already in. Now he's working on taking over. If you want to prevent this by leaving right away or if you want to prepare for it by implementing a plan for your own life (see Survival Tip #14), that's something for you to consider and think about. But whichever way you decide to proceed, KNOW THIS:

Your husband IS getting worse (see Tip # 7) and there WILL be a point of no return.

Or perhaps I should say, no escape.

A Sioux creation story says that long ago the Creator gathered all of Creation and said, "I want to hide something from the humans until they are ready for it. It is the realization that they create their own reality.

The eagle said, "Give it to me, I will take it to the moon."

The Creator said, "No. One day they will go there and find it."

The salmon said, "I will bury it on the bottom of the ocean."

"No, they will go there too."

The buffalo said, "I will bury in on the Great Plains."

The Creator said, "They will cut into the skin of the Earth and find it even there."

Grandmother Mole, who lives in the breast of Mother Earth, and who has no physical eyes but sees with spiritual eyes, said, "Put it inside of them."

And the Creator said, "It is done."

SURVIVAL TIP #16

Create Your Own Reality

(Or Risk Having Your Alcoholic Husband Create It For You)

It's November 14, 2015 and I was just finishing up this book when last night Paris was attacked horrifically, with nothing short of pure vile and evil, by terrorists. In all honestly, I think what I am about to write was already percolating around in my brain but the tragic news out of France has solidified it for me.

IT IS LIFE SUCKING, SOUL NUMBING, AND HEART BREAKING TO BE MARRIED TO AN ALCOHOLIC.

It's hard to overstate the magnitude of trying to live your life while married to a man that thinks nothing of calling you a "fucking bitch," telling you to "go fucking die" and spends the majority of his life destroying it – and those around him - with alcohol. Making it all the more difficult and heartbreaking is the fact that, at some point in your life anyway, you chose this man as someone to share your life with. You invited him into your life and accepted the invitation into his. You believed that the two of you were forming an exclusive team to take on the world together. A team that would love, honor and respect one another if and when (especially when) the world at large was hell-bent on knocking you down and running your over. And indeed, he may very well have been that man who loved, honor and respect.

That is, before the mind-boggling insanity known as alcoholism staged a coup and took over his being.

Alcoholism will take the man you once trusted and counted on, the man you once saw as your equal, your partner, your protector and turn him into someone you won't even recognize. Someone you can't trust, can't count on and who you will need protection – be it physical, emotional or mental - *from*. Someone who will tear you down far quicker and with a profundity of spite and malice seemingly unparalleled in the outside world.

Being married to an alcoholic is one of The Biggies and life will toss it at you as effortlessly as your grandpa flipping you a quarter.

It is no minor thing, that's for sure.

But then neither is having someone you love killed in a terrorist attack as they sit at an outdoor café in Paris, enjoying a picturesque autumn night.

Or having your leg blown off in Afghanistan.

Or being diagnosed with Lou Gehrig's disease at age 40.

Or losing your entire family to a freak accident, like a plane crashing into your house.

Or watching your son or daughter spend the rest of his/her life in a wheelchair.

The list goes on and on AND ON. Life doles out some hard, bad, tough, painful beyond words, STUFF for us to deal with while we enjoy free rides around the sun.

It HURTS to be married to an alcoholic. I know! I'm living it. Alcoholism is a wicked, multi-barbed, little son-of-a-bitch webble that burrows itself into every fiber of your being and every moment of your life. On a regular, daily basis your life is being negatively affected and impacted by your husband's compulsive drinking and his accompaning behavior. And this is all just while your husband is a reasonably functioning alcoholic.

If you're still with your husband as he draws closer and closer to being an end-stage alcoholic, the impact on your life will be near-cataclysmic. In addition to - over and above that is - "just" the behavior of

83

the alcoholic, you are now dealing with the issues of physically caring for a very sick individual. And not just any individual. Not someone who simply grew old and her body is giving out. Not an individual who was hit by enemy fire while half-way across the world defending our freedoms. Not someone who is suffering from a terminal or chronic illness due to nothing more than the (bad) luck of life's draw. No, if you're still with your husband when he reaches end-stage, you're going to be the caregiver to someone who made the choice day after day after day FOR A VERY LONG TIME, despite the reality of what he was doing to himself, to continue to drink. And now YOU have to hold the pieces together?

Living with an alcoholic husband makes you want to CURL UP IN A BALL and let the world go by. Do you know what someone who is lost in the woods and being threatened by hypothermia must do? She must - must, must, must, MUST - keep moving. Sleep calls to her; demands of her. She may become so exhausted and cold that every fiber of her being is begging her to lay down and "rest." But the wise woodswoman knows that to sleep is to die. If she lays down, her body will succumb to the cold.

In the same way, as the wife of an alcoholic, you must not stop moving. You must not give into the cries of your heart and soul to rest, to stop, to give up the fight. When you are married to an alcoholic, eventually it comes down to, literally, ONLY TWO POSSIBLE OUTCOMES:

You either succumb to the "cold" and die - be it physically, emotionally, mentally, and/or spiritually...

Or you don't.

Because if you heed nothing else, heed this:

THE BEAST OF ALCOHOLISM TAKES NO PRISONERS.

There is no neutral in this war. No status quo. No Switzerland.

Just as the alcoholic is progressively getting worse, your being, your sense of self - Your Very Soul - is being progressively destroyed by life with an alcoholic husband.

YOUR LIFE IS BEING ERODED AWAY.

This is not hyperbole on my part.

I can feel how far I have fallen myself from who I once was. I know I have lost much of all I valued and even admired in myself. I heard a woman sum up poetically and perfectly the effects a man's drinking has on his wife. She said,

"I have lost so much of me in the anger. I have lost some of the very best parts of me."

Make no mistake, let me not mince words in the least: YOU ARE BEING DESTROYED BY HIS DRINKING!

And so your choice is simple.

You either look the Beast of Alcoholism in the eye and say,

"Not me! Not my soul! You may have his, but you're not getting mine!"

Or you don't.

IT REALLY IS THAT CLEAR CUT.

I am telling you.

You have to fight.

And you have to fight when the last thing you want to do is fight. When you feel like your husband's drinking is beckoning you to lay down and rest. When you feel like you don't even have the energy to lift your head up, much less put one foot in front of the other and propel yourself forward so that you might stumble out of the dark woods of someone else's compulsive drinking.

I know what you're thinking.

You're thinking, "Ok, Mrs. Smarty Pants, just HOW am I supposed to fight this Beast if you are so certain I should and I can."

Well, I don't know.

That's right, I don't really know the specifics of how you are going to fight this Beast but I can give you the basics. I have to warn you though; these suggestions may sound like something right out of a Dr. Phil show or Oprah special. They'll probably even sound a bit like a generic New Year's Resolution list. Oversimplified and obvious. And you know why that is? (No, not because I'm a shameless plagiarizer.)

It's because the things Dr. Phil or Oprah says, the things your best friend tells you, what your therapist says are or the words you whisper to yourself every December 31 are a) pretty much the same message just delivered in different words by different people and b) what really works.

YOU HAVE TO CREATE A LIFE FOR YOURSELF.

A life that is yours physically, emotionally, spiritually and FINANCIALLY.

Your husband's alcoholism is running and controlling your life right now, even if it seems as though he never does any more than sit in the garage/basement/family room/living room night after night and get drunk? His alcoholism has infiltrated and compromised the very foundation of your life. So the first thing you need to do is create a new infrastructure or foundation from which to live your life.

Start by striving to live in a way that honors and supports who you are as a living, breathing human being with the innate right to lead a life free from hostility, anger and turmoil. (Because alcoholism pretty much tells you on a daily basis that you are NOT a living, breathing human being with the innate right to live a life free from hostility, anger and turmoil). So, a few suggestions:

Give up eating crap food. Just like the next one (start exercising) is not about obtaining the unattainable body, this isn't about dieting your way into "skinny jeans" or a "size 0." Give up the crap food because it does not nourish your body or your soul. You're at war. You need to eat to sustain your strength - the physical as well as the spiritual. Besides, if you're living with an alcoholic there is a good chance you are using food the same way the alcoholic is using alcohol. I know I was! I'd be awake at all hours of the

86

morning, chowing down on whatever sugary or salty - or preferably sugary-salty - crap I could find in the cupboard. Besides "helping" me to maintain an extra 50 pounds(!!), my own addictive behavior left me feeling hopeless and bad about myself and, frankly, a little bit of a hypocrite. If I was expecting my husband to give up his chemical crutch, why couldn't I give up mine? Food is addicting. Living with an alcoholic husband sucks. Break the habit of using one to survive the other.

Start exercising. Not exercising like "I need to have the body of a Victoria Secret model" but exercising like walking in the morning or swimming laps or any sort of physical movement you can commit to and sustain for at least 30 minutes. (Walking really is the ideal exercise!) There is much healing, insight, clarity and direction to be garnished from movement. The mind needs the body to move in order to be at its strongest. Not to mention all those sweet endorphins that get released through exercise. (Which it should be noted those endorphins are the same thing your alcoholic husband's brain releases through his drinking. And you, if you're eating compulsively, get the benefit of via Twinkies, glazed doughnuts and/or Big Macs. Just saying...) You don't have to train for a marathon or go all "CrossFit." Just. Move. You might even find an exercise or class that you (believe it or not!) come to enjoy! Imagine that! That would be pure gold for your psyche as well as your soul and your body!

You should journal. Writing is very cathartic. Remember that old joke about how does a "Thermos" bottle know whether to keep the contents hot or cold? Writing is sort of like that. The act of writing something down can solidify it within you and make it a part of you forever.

Or it can help you release it!

I don't know how writing "knows" when to do which but it does.

You definitely need to meditate. You definitely do not need to learn how to do it "right." This isn't about training with a meditation-guru or finding a Buddhist monastery to meditate at. Oh sure, there are monks who can still their minds so completely as to sit "idle" for hours at a time. This is neither what you are after or what you need. Just 15 minutes or so a day of meditation - simply stilling your body and quieting your mind best you can will do amazing things for you throughout for you throughout the entire day.

TRY MAKING SOME ART!! Art is so cathartic, a natural part of who human beings are and a too-often overlooked tool for dealing with life. Most people think they have to "be" an artist or at least "be" good at making art in order to justify spending time making art! Do art because human beings are innately creative creatures (yes, even you!) and anything that can help you reconnect with your innate human-being-ness is a powerful ally to have in this battle for your being! Picasso said, "Art cleanses the daily grime of life from our souls." No one has need for a cleansing of life's daily grime more than the wife of an alcoholic. Go to Michael's or Target, buy a pad of paper and some pencils. Or get crayons (who DOESN'T love the smell of crayons!) and a coloring book. Adult coloring books are all the rage now. One more thing, don't even entertain, for one millisecond, the notion that you need to "make money" with your art! (Unless an artist's life is long what you have felt a calling to pursue!)

CHALLENGE YOURSELF! This is probably one of the most powerful things you can do for yourself - as well as the most difficult! There is immense power and personal growth in pushing yourself beyond your mental, emotional and/or physical comfort zones!

I just signed up for a ballet class!! Yes, BALLET! No, I was not a dancer in my younger days. In fact, I HAVE NEVER TAKEN A DANCE CLASS IN MY LIFE! And I'll probably look like the aforementioned elephant in a tutu (see Tip #8) in my ballet garb but ballet has always intrigued me (I have at least been to the ballet). Like a secret, alter ego I marvel at the strength and dedication of the ballet dancer, her feet as ugly as her craft is beautiful. And while I'm pretty sure I've missed the window for making prima ballerina, ballet class will be an hour where I won't even have the time (or desire) to think about my alcoholic husband.

Turn on some music -- just something gentle and calm playing during the day.

Definitely go outside! It's amazing how we can forget to go outside when dealing and living with an alcoholic. And amazing how cleansing the act can be!

READ LOTS OF BOOKS. Not "about" alcoholics per say though those can have their place and offer some guidance. But also about life and change and goals and happiness. Pursue happiness and freedom like a scholar pursues her field of study. Infuse your life with the teachings of great writers, teachers and spiritual beings. Find a way to get outside the alcoholic world you've been involuntarily dragged into.

When you are married to an alcoholic, it comes down to this: you have to seek a higher level of consciousness and being. It is easy - SO EASY - for your mind to get locked in a loop of continuous and repetitive thoughts that center on the alcoholic, his drinking and his behavior. I'm not talking about "codependency" (because I vehemently oppose that accusation!) but rather the pure inevitability of your mind getting stuck on the pain, turmoil and chaos of being married to an alcoholic when it is bombarded, on a daily basis, with the pain, turmoil and chaos... of being married to an alcoholic.

How could these thoughts not become your mind's "default setting?" You have to re-set your mind. You have to get outside these thoughts, outside yourself, outside the alcoholism and bring in fresh thoughts, fresh insights, fresh experiences, fresh things for your mind to settle on, think about and marvel at so that it can interrupt the Alcoholic Loop.

(One of) the great ironies of being married to an alcoholic is that it presents some of life's richest and most fertile soil in which to sow your dreams. I recently started seeing a therapist and she asked me what I hoped to get from therapy. I said,

"I want to be able to say that I took the worst thing in my life - my husband's drinking - and use it to create the best life of my dreams."

War with the Beast of Alcoholism is not for the squeamish or faint of heart. It's certainly not a war you volunteered for. You were conscripted into this army. But now that you're in it, you have little choice but to fight. It's You against The Beast. One of you is going to win and one of you is going to die.

Which one will you be?

You were born with goodness and trust.

You were born with ideals and dreams.

You were born with greatness.

You were born with wings.

You are not meant for crawling, so don't.

You have wings.

Learn to use them and fly.

Rumi

NOTES

Stop acting so small. You are the universe in ecstatic motion.

Rumi

NOTES

If you want to conquer the anxiety of life, live in the moment. Live in the breath.

Amit Ray, Om Chanting and Meditation

NOTES

Your blessings lay beyond your fear.

Shannon L. Adler

NOTES

You have power over your mind – not outside events. Realize this and you will find your strength.

Marcus Aurelius, Meditations

NOTES

In the depth of winter, I finally learned within me lay an invincible summer.

Albert Camus

CONTACT

Please visit me at my blog, QuietRagingWaters.com

And if you are so inclined, you may email me at:
tahprimer@gmail.com